THE QUIET ANSWER

THE QUIET ANSWER

Hugh Prather

A DOLPHIN BOOK
Doubleday, New York

Library of Congress Cataloging in Publication Data

Prather, Hugh.
  The quiet answer.

  "A Dolphin book."
  1. Spiritual life.   I. Title.
BL624.P697   291.4   AACR2

Library of Congress Catalog Card Number: 80-2979
ISBN 0-385-17605-8

Copyright © 1982 by Hugh Prather

9   8

Out of love for its Source,
I dedicate this book to
A Course in Miracles

A Course in Miracles is published by The Foundation for
Inner Peace, Box 635, Tiburon, California   94920

All you need do is make the effort to learn, for the Holy Spirit has a unified goal for effort. If different abilities are applied long enough to one goal, the abilities themselves become unified.

A Course in Miracles

To be in the Kingdom is merely to focus your full attention on it.

A Course in Miracles

Thou wilt keep him in perfect peace whose mind is stayed on Thee.

The Bible

CONTENTS

TO THE READER:

Nothing in this book is meant to disturb you. Mere controversy is never truly helpful. But love is. If you find yourself in disagreement with something I have said, please laugh happily and forgive me my ignorance. God has not finished with me yet.

My purpose in writing this book is to attempt to provide you with a number of immediate and practical ways to return to God's peace. It is therefore not necessary to begin at the beginning and read straight through. You may prefer to work from the Table of Contents or simply open the pages at random.

Although the purpose of this book is peace, if peace is not the alternative you seek, all you need do is ask yourself what you do want. The more specific you are, the more quickly you will free yourself, because, above all else, the ego you have made does not want you to concentrate. If you see clearly the gift it is offering you, you simply will not want it. That is why you need never fear your desires or run from your fantasies.

Fear is a distraction. It is mental turmoil. It does not focus. It does not even know exactly what it fears. Fear is pure avoidance without direction. Calmness dispells fear by restoring the willingness to look. Through either direct or gradual means, the thoughts and exercises in this book urge you to look, to be honest, to be calm, so that the grounds for happiness can be clearly seen. And these grounds will never be comparative. True gratitude is not based on the perception that others have less or suffer more. It is the recognition that spirit instead of flesh holds all that is of value and that there is no end to spirit. Because love does exist, you are free.

Hugh Prather
March 8, 1981
Santa Fe, New Mexico

ASSUMPTIONS
OF THIS BOOK

There are two levels of perception. The first is like a dream. The second reflects only Love. We can always tell which of these we are using by how we feel. For even though there may be occasions when we like a dream, we will always sense the ground of anxiety from which it rises. In contrast, when we are perceiving accurately, we feel a deep and freeing peace and a certainty about the outcome of all things.

At the start of our journey, the perception of love may appear to come and quickly go. And for some there may be long periods of comparative bleakness. Yet beneath it will be a growing sense of gentleness and innocence and a deepening conviction that a Friend walks beside us and holds our hand in love.

It eventually becomes clear that we have not been abandoned by Reality but only chose to look away awhile. Now we begin to see that everything is up to us because nothing external exists that can attack us and deprive us of our Home in the Heart of God.

What then must we do to wake to the recognition that the journey is over because Reality has never been changed? We need merely open our eyes. Instead of beginning still another useless search for small advantages, we must look honestly at the nature of what changes constantly, for it is empty and meaningless and very sad.

And it can only be imagined in darkness. In its place we must choose Reality, not only because it is fair to all but because it is a simple fact, and the only one there is. To recognize Love as real is to never again want a compromise decision. We turn from the world we made, from all it seemed to hold out to us but never relinquished, and from all it appeared to do to us that we have not revenged. We withdraw from that useless, endless fight and accept instead a freedom without limit. We turn and face the Light. No more than this. And if we find we have not freed ourselves completely, we practice awhile longer only what will make a difference: Charity without identification with pain. Gentleness that is consistent. And happiness that is not snatched and is not hidden.

Each time we practice love, we open our eyes a little further on the Place of Love. Love is our means, our end, our Home, our Family, and our Identity. That evidence alone, seen and felt, will show the emptiness of dreams. But if we treat the means of our awaking as a trinket, something merely to be worn occasionally like some clever adornment, it will have no deep meaning for us and cannot disclose its limitless worth.

Pull your decision to walk straight into God around every part of you and over every instant of your day and night. Exclude no one and no thing. Make it the thought you wake with and the goal you cherish in your sleep. See no other person without light, and light will begin to pervade each crack and corner of your surroundings, until you recognize clearly that you have never left the Place where God watches over you who are His child, His meaning, and His joy.

ESSAYS OF
ENCOURAGEMENT

POTENTIAL

Is it not true that you have something of value to offer? Haven't you seen some evidence in your life of your potential to give a gift that will gladden the heart of someone else? Haven't you been kind? Haven't you uplifted? Haven't you helped someone at some time to not feel isolated and misunderstood? And is that potential in you not worth your effort to release more fully? If what you now think you are does not call to you for consistency, what you could be should. Your potential is love. And love is of God. To consistently make others happy will do far more than make you happy. It will release the world from pain and turn hell into heaven for every living thing. Your potential as a healer has no point beyond which it cannot go.

WISDOM

This is the lesson. This is all that is being
learned. Forgiveness truly is the key to
happiness, to simple liking, to heartfelt contentment, and to the certainty we will exist
forever in freedom. Just forgive, merely let go
of dislike and "justified" resentments, simply
forget grievances and bleak anticipations, set all
things free of memories and cruel expectations,
let loose, let go, let be, and the earth cannot
help but sing and your heart dance with it.
Forgive and be happy. That is the ancient
secret, the inner teaching, the hidden answer,
the lost knowledge, the only message of the
still, quiet voice, the only wisdom ever to be at-
tained.

CONTROL

I turn from what I cannot improve to what I can. If I cannot heal my body, I **can** lose interest in being sick. I alone choose what preoccupies me. There is no doubt that thought can be turned to either love or fear. I can choose not to endlessly trace the "causes" of my difficulties and project onto the future their limitations and pains. If I cannot make this person stop condemning me, I can fail to analyze his motives and rest from defending my actions, because my mind will build a case for universal innocence as easily as it will look for personal guilt. No matter what appearances I dislike, I can turn from wearying attempts to tinker them into perfection. Let me begin with what can be changed this instant. My mind can open to the light of God. And within Its soft appeal what cannot be seen with kindness?

LOVE

Love is natural and should be habitual and universal in its application. Discrete or focused love is not love but only the ego's substitute. Love should be as effortless as breathing and as indiscriminate as falling snow. Love is what naturally happens when the mind is attempting no shift or change. Love is a state of mind or a vision that handles all things equally. There is no part of love that can be privately kept, and the attempt to use love to hold our "own" merely reflects a misunderstanding of its nature. Love can only accompany what is given away, and since all of love must be given in order for all of it to remain, there can be no range to our giving. There is only one kind of love, the uncalculated kind.

JUDGING

Today I will allow all things to be. I will judge nothing. I am willing for the weather to be whatever it is. I am content to have each encounter that is to come. Nor will I resist the circumstances in which I am placed. I will let my friends act however they will. I will not remain with one word spoken or a single gesture or act. Instead, I will release my attention from censure to rest on this gentle moment. I will allow each member of my family to be what he is, without **defining** what he is. I will attempt to see my children as they are, without interpretations drawn from my experience and free of motivations I have attributed to myself. I will not assign my spouse's role or function or attitude toward me. I will not cherish a wish for a shift in personality or habits, nor will I try to push anyone in a direction by moderating my joy or withholding my normal responses. I will let all people be just as they are today, and in this stillness of thought I will ask what God sees in each one, that He made him His own beloved child.

FANTASIZING

What has a reasonable chance of giving me simple happiness within this instant? Imagining future arms of flesh, or visualizing the present and willing arms of Love? Fantasizing future riches, or pausing to sense the deep and endless wealth of my Core? Planning little triumphs over others, or picturing what caring and joy could pass between me and some living thing? Isn't one kind use of my mind a more practical act than a thousand vain imaginings? Why do I fill my thoughts with scenes and plans that, even if they occurred, would not make me feel complete or even gratify me for more than a little while, when I could spend this very moment attempting something peaceful and lastingly enjoyable? When will I accept the soft truth of this moment and recognize the thorough falsity of my thoughts about tomorrow?

DISGUISES

We often hurt ourselves as a means of teaching ourselves "lessons." That is why we find it difficult to believe there is Something that does not use pain as a teaching aid. And that is also why we are so deeply suspicious of the motives of everyone. Yet this suspicion must at least be **questioned** if we are ever to allow ourselves to hear the instructions we are being given. There is indeed a Hand held out to us in love. It will never be withdrawn. We have been assured of this more than once. The universe simply does not have anything up its sleeve. And God does not spank your hands to teach you love.

THINKING

Thoughts cannot separate themselves from the
mind that thinks them, and that is why I cannot
succeed in dismissing another person. If I have
thought of him, he is mine. What then do I wish
to make of this piece of my mind? A garden or
a slaughterhouse? My mind holds everything in
a vast circle of pure spirit. I cannot think a dis-
turbing thought without requesting that everything share in my distress. And I cannot be at
peace without offering peace to the entire world
that peoples my thought. Because listening is
love, love can be transmitted through silence as
easily as through words and deeds. And without
love, there are no deeds, and no communication
has actually taken place.

BEGINNING

If I am unwilling to let this problem go completely, let me at least loosen my grip a little. I will create some softness around the edges by stepping aside and waiting a moment for another point of view to come to me. I will allow a small measure of Christ's gentleness into my mind. At least I will let my mind consider a moment's peaceful rest, if not a happy laugh of relief. Love Itself is what calls to me to give myself rest. It is **not** humble to remain in turmoil, and Love does not ask this of me. I will reach for one peaceful thought. And I will feel God's support of this endeavor.

KNOWING

It is in my refusal to make decisions about my life, any decision at all, that I open my mind to quiet correction and gentle instruction. I must be firm in my knowledge that I do not know anything. This is the one thing I do know. My ego will not be the part of my mind that will wake me from this nightmare. Whatever about me is agitated holds no hope. It is far better for me to take time to remember that there is nothing for me to decipher, than to use time considering what I should do. I am not in a position to calculate my own improvement. Therefore, let me be still and patiently wait for Love's Voice. It will do more than just direct me. To hear God's Call is to be literally encompassed in His Gentleness. The place described is the Place. To hear it spoken of is to be included in It within the same instant. What is of God is God.

INTERPRETING

Because nothing I see holds a solitary, perma-
nent meaning, I am free to give it whatever
meaning I wish. How do I want to interpret what
another person does? What might anyone do
that could not in fairness be seen as at least a
plea for understanding? If I question the overall
validity of my personal tastes and judgments,
my first reaction to another's behavior is also
called into question. A given tone of voice, a
particular set of the face or body, the use of certain words, can now mean whatever I choose to
hear and see. So I will allow a new description
to form in my mind. Even if in the beginning I
do not feel the truth of the words, I will begin to
softly sing them deep within. The world I see is
not solid and immovable, and I am not insane to
deny its dark assertions. In doing so, I seek not
to change the way things look but rather to
make a new reading with my heart. For I am at
liberty to notice God's Hand in everything that
occurs.

VISION

What I see with my body's eyes alone is not happening. What I see with love is real. As a lampshade surrounds a light, so things appear to encircle spirit, and words imprison thought. But that appearance of limitation is only imagined. Spirit is invisible to the body's eyes and cannot be heard with ears alone, and yet sounds and objects begin to brighten as I focus my spiritual sight. I simply say, "I love you," to everything, and mean it, and all the gauzy lampshades on earth begin to vanish before a world of immeasurable beauty and light. Extend only kindnesses to this world, and there will be no reason to look for signs of vengeance. I cannot be afraid after a moment of harmlessness.

MIND

Objects are seen through eyes, not with eyes. Reality is seen with love, not through it. This is because only the mind sees, and only the mind is love. To ask, "What am I doing with my mind?" is to question everything that needs to be questioned. When I am **truly** thinking, God is the Mind with which I think. And there is no Mind possible but Love. All else is mere hallucination, or absentmindedness, and can be safely neglected and forgotten for good. God is all there is. There is nothing else. All I need do is see only Him. An open heart sees only God.

PRAYING

We do not speak into space or into another's
ears. On that level nothing is actually said or
heard. To be of real help we must speak into the
Place of God. It is a Place encircled by holiness
and filled with the soft atmosphere of peace. We
speak quietly into stillness. Peacefully, we extend pure peace. There is a place where you will
speak today. There is a peace into which you
will go. What you are listening for is a softening
of your heart and a sweetening of your mind.
The gentle voice of love moves quietly through
you and out into the world.

DESIRES

If I know what the end results will be, even if only intellectually, why continue to be dishonest with myself? If all external pursuits lead to distress, then I have not in truth discovered an exception. Therefore, let me quickly release my mind from the deception that any desire at all could take me to a place I would want to be. A desire for future good is merely a denial made in the present. Bodies and things, careers and sacrifices are not desirable in themselves because I am already whole. Consequently, I do not need to know the "right" people or be in the "right" places. There are none. Nor will I achieve a degree of contentment from withdrawal and isolation. I am already one Self created purely of Love, a perfect Song in heaven, a Child of God loved without limit, and an indistinguishable part of Him. Why then spend one second more pursuing what can only make me feel small and cut off, a thing in need of constant fixes and half-hearted charities, an inconvenience to itself and others? If I know this sorry self-image will never be successfully enhanced, why try? Let me not seek one thing more on behalf of my ego.

REST

The answer comes in only one size, yet it will fit all problems. All problems are equally easy or difficult to solve. They are either all easy or all difficult depending on my present willingness to stand by and listen. Why am I not relieved to know that all God wants of me is to be happy? Is this to be called a demand or a gift? Love cannot work through me if I am sad and pre-occupied with a hundred meaningless concerns. All He asks is that I lean gently on Him awhile. Nothing more. All He requests is that I take His hand, and His counsel, and rest for one happy moment in Him.

MIRACLES

Love works miracles. Yet what do I choose to emphasize—the miracle or the love? If I shift my attention to the miracle, I lose sight of its Cause. What is important is important, and what is only secondary is not deserving of delay.

BEING RIGHT

Have I just composed the rules for my happiness? Have I set the conditions and described
the necessary course of events that this day
must provide? And am I now proving that I am
right by being unhappy because today is not
proceeding as I have imagined it should? Let me
give up being right so I may gain being happy.
Then let me say this: "I release this day from all
my demands. I ask nothing of this day at all. I
will settle deep into now and wish all living
things well."

GUILT

One obvious reason I do not want to spend time feeling guilty is that, as a channel for Love, my mind is either open or closed to Love's yearning to reach out through me and make others deeply happy. Guilt keeps it closed and so continues the original error. To wait in peace opens my mind by removing the blockage of fear. Do I, in fact, honor my God in what He wills to do? Then let me stop interfering so that He may show through me how deeply He loves and how unfailingly He cares for His children. Guilt simply does not honor and appreciate and so does not heal anything.

LINES OF THOUGHT

Today I will make a consistent attempt to fail to think along the lines suggested by this dream. I will not fantasize by inventing little scenarios based on the assumption that some parts of illusions have importance. Any aspect of a dream is unworthy of speculation, and whatever is without love is merely a dream. Instead, I will think, recall, anticipate, reason only along lines suggested by fairness and freedom. Today I will not idly deceive myself, but will watch over my mind to keep it a bright and enjoyable source of experience, and use it only in ways that will honor me and my God.

PURPOSES

I am continually assigning a purpose to my use of time. This cannot be avoided at my stage of learning. What can be redirected is the purpose itself. Either I am assigning the ego's ever-changing and conflicting series of small purposes, or the one purpose that sees everyone's interests as the same. My unified purpose for using time includes no wish for thoughts that could not be shared by anyone with all of his heart. What is this moment **for**? Let me not be afraid to ask.

USING TIME

All things appear to me to happen in time. But that does not mean they happen because of time. Time heals nothing, and to wait on time to relieve pain or to mend betrayals does not put my time to good use. Yet time is always put to some use. How valuable I believe I am determines what that use will be. If my present attitude is that I am of little meaning, I will not be inclined to assign a high value to my time. I am not worth the time I have, and so I use time to prove my insignificance and ineffectuality. This my ego calls "humility." I rumble around within each moment and bounce haphazardly and hopelessly off every change time brings. However, if I use time well, then I **am** worthy. I can recognize my place within reality merely by attempting to make good use of each instant. Now I see my place by being it. With every moment I refuse to withdraw from His Attitude, I raise my estimate of my part in God's plan.

GIFTS

The little breaks I take from pain, my periods of rest and quiet meditation, are gifts I give myself and everyone I have ever known. I am only doing the enjoyable, nothing more. My wish is simply to think thoughts that make me happy and to rest from those barren of love. Let me imagine a world I would truly like to be part of, because my effort is serving to bring it about. Let me remember always that it is not my duty to pray, it is my fond pleasure.

RESOLVE

I will not begin again until I can feel the strength in my resolve. For the rest of this day my goal is a quantitative one. I will make a new effort to bring more aspects of my life to sanity than I have ever done before. I will renew my purpose frequently, and I will remind myself that whenever I allow my goal to be the same as God's, it cannot fail. The world I see through my body's eyes has nothing I could possibly use. I will not be deceived that some part of it has suddenly become substantial. I will try harder today. That much at least is within my control. I will try for release from worry and for loving kindness in place of irritation and cold resistance. I will try for simple understanding, for an even-handed and innocent vision. I will try for a day of continuing peace and effortless doing, that my mind may extend a blanket of quietness over every place and happening I see. And should my heart again become angry or unyielding, as quickly as possible I will return to Love's way and my true will.

GRIEVANCES

I release you from my hurt feelings. I free you from my reading of your motives. I withdraw my "justified" outrage and leave you clean and happy in my mind. In place of censure, I offer you all of God's deep contentment and peace. I will perceive you singing, with a soft smile of freedom and a glow of rich satisfaction. I bless you my brother. You are a shining member of the Family of God, and I will wait patiently for this truthful vision to come honestly to my mind.

LISTENING

I give this time to You alone. Please guide me in
this prayer. I ask only for honesty and total
sincerity. May I pray from my heart alone. If
there is anything I should experience now, or
any words I should hear, I am ready to receive
them. In stillness and quiet listening, I now open
myself to You.

EMPTINESS

Now I lay down the past hour and the past days.
Many times I have forgotten what is important
and have lifted what is unimportant to a position of prominence in my mind. But regretting
that is not my purpose now. I release myself
from all thoughts of guilt and failing. I let all
witnesses to instability and weakness be still.
Empty of the past, I turn to You. I know nothing
now, not even about myself. Fill me completely
with Your Heart.

BLEAKNESS

These thoughts will not go away, so I pause now
and give them to You. I have been making a
real effort to ask for peace, and yet I am clearly
not at peace. You have said that all I need do is
ask sincerely. Don't my efforts alone show that I
am sincere in wanting to let go of this bleakness
and see instead Your Beauty in everyone? There
seems to be some catch in all of this. If a little
willingness is all that is needed, haven't I
already done my part many times over? I have
been still, and the distress has continued. I have
tried to listen and have heard nothing. I am ex-
hausted in both doing and not doing. So I fail. I
fail in You. I give up completely. I stumble and
fall into You.

EXCEPTIONS

I want to see You everywhere so that in all
honesty I may love what I see. That my mind
may be a place of rest, I want You a part of each
consideration, every wish and meaning. I will affirm no law that is not fair, no rule that cannot
set anything free, no condition that does not
embrace in honor or enfold in safety and peace.
Seen wherever I look, acknowledged wherever
my thought turns, heard in every remark and
any sound at all, be You my universe, my One
Self, my All.

COMPLETE

You are the breath that inspires me. The food
That nourishes and gratifies. Yours is
The mind with which I pray, and Yours the life
By which I live. Your peace leads me to heal.
Yours are the thoughts I offer all in love.
You open wide my eyes and guide my feet.
You still my anxious heart. You are my love,
My Father, and my Self. I recognize
All others in Your Face. You are the Friend
In all my friends, my one relationship.
You are my rest and my Identity.
You are but all there is. I am complete in You.

A THIRTY-DAY
COURSE

Affirmation: "Because God is with me, I am content to be wherever I am."

Guide: Anytime I feel distress today, I will remind myself it is no accident I am wherever I am. And I am glad to be here because God holds me in His love. Anytime I feel a twinge of longing, I will ask myself if it is likely that God misunderstands my question. And I will return my mind to trust.

Affirmation: "What do I want this to mean?"

Guide: I am free to see God's gentle lesson emerge from all that happens today. To do this, I will practice letting go of my first reaction and allow love to be added to my second. If something does not please me, I will gently question the meaning I have given it and substitute instead a meaning as peaceful as God's.

Affirmation: "I forget what to be angry about."

Guide: Who has not looked back on an argu-
ment only to recognize he has forgotten what
it was about? I can forget all conflict, even in
these present circumstances. And any other
"cause" of suffering. Within each new situation, I will remember that although my ego
set it up, God anticipated it and assigned His
gentle purpose to every aspect. Now its only
purpose is to make me happy. So I will mentally lean back and **let** it make me happy. Sorrow ends in laughter and anger ends in love,
and all this weary world will end when I am no
longer afraid to be happy.

Affirmation: "All released . . . all is peace."

Guide: As I release everything from darkening
recollections and from visions of uncaring
"laws," I behold all living things at peace,
lovely, and completely safe in God's care.
Today's affirmation can be used in rhythm
with breathing. Or I can picture its meaning
everywhere as a means of calming my mind.
And it is indeed a proper blessing for anyone I
am tempted to condemn. I release the world,
and my gift is peace.

Affirmation: "Guilt is the same mistake in
another form. To bless
is my decision."

Guide: Thoughts of guilt are a declaration that
one of Love's own children has been damaged
by me. Can this possibly help the one I believe I have attacked? I will bless him instead.
And affirm my changelessness as well. My
new response to any mistake I recognize today will be to offer thoughts of love rather
than to withhold my blessing by pursuing
thoughts of guilt.

Affirmation: "My body is a means of communicating love."

Guide: My ego uses the body to make others feel separate. Love uses it to make them happy. I will begin with the times I recognize that I am putting my body to some use. This use I will quietly examine. If it is not to make others feel secure, peaceful, and cared for, I will acknowledge how small and anxious a thing I also have become in my own eyes, and I will pick instead some gentle thought to let my body pass along.

Affirmation: "To gain the position of freedom, I will step back to the position of love."

Guide: In the various situations that arise today, my ego will offer me two options: winning or losing. God will offer me a third: equality. Competitiveness is a request for pain because it questions the fairness of God's love, in which no one is slighted. Within equality is only freedom, for in true equality all limits are renounced for all. Today I will reject a position of advantage so I may practice the position of perfection.

Affirmation: "I will let no idle thought continue undismissed."

Guide: All idle thoughts contain elements of attack and are therefore a request that reality include limits on freedom. No thought is neutral. Either I am choosing a thought containing love or one devoid of it. That choice is my only concern today and the sole determiner of what I experience.

Affirmation: "If I choose peace, I will not be at peace alone."

Guide: Nor can I fear alone. Whatever thought I think, every person in this world thinks with me. Not in form, but in content. I will stop long enough today to let this fact have its effect on my thought selection. Each time I decide for comfort, let me picture someone else relaxing at this same instant. To save from pain is my only function.

Affirmation: "I will pause frequently for instruction today."

Guide: There is no step so small that I would not improve my chances for happiness by listening an instant before I proceed. God has given me His Mind.

Affirmation: "Let my first step be stillness."

Guide: How can I expect love's interpretation to enter a mind that loudly insists on another view? How can I feel God's deep peace while I angrily judge everything around me? No matter what the source of my complaint, or from what direction affliction seems to come, my inward reaction today will be gently to do nothing. The Christ in me is very quiet; my ego is very restless; therefore I will choose the way of peace.

Affirmation: "Learning to respond to now is all there is to learn."

Guide: Each instant I remember, I will take a closer look at this present moment and all it contains. The journey to God is the journey into now. To ascend into Heaven is to sink so deeply into now that I lose all interest in the past and future. The ego was and will be, but only God **is**.

Affirmation: "Today there is nothing to decide."

Guide: Because there is a Plan, nothing remains to be decided. The answer has been given, my way has been set, and my Guide provided. A thousand times today, I will fall back in the Hands of God. And if any question arises, I will simply say, "You decide," and know that it is done.

Affirmation: "Help is not being forced on me."

Guide: Help lies gently on my mind waiting only for my invitation to enter. I will not be coerced or tricked into the state of Mind that is Heaven, for every step I take is at my bidding. Happiness is the choice I must make, and fear the only sacrifice. To any sign of resistance I will say, "Help is not being forced on me."

Affirmation: "My will is not threatened by God's. To hear His will is to recognize my own."

Guide: God knows what I will enjoy. It is not His plan to hurt me. Can I by myself see **all** the outcomes of the least of my idle wishes? Then let me not presume a conflict that does not exist. It is His pleasure to carry me through the lawns of Heaven and to set me down by the quiet waters of His Peace. Instead of trusting uninformed imaginings, I will practice listening only to my heart today, knowing it tells me of God's will and of my own.

Affirmation: "I will make no effort to step ahead of God."

Guide: If the ocean was pure mind and I was a wave, I would be in terror if I tried to distinguish myself from the water that produced me. What is a wave without water, and what is a mind without God? My ego endlessly searches for ways to set itself apart from others and become "self" sufficient. But I will be still and remember where I am.

Affirmation: "If I wish any change in the surface, I cannot see beyond it."

Guide: My body's eyes show me the surface of things, yet Love looks past form into pure peace. To choose to do whatever I am doing and to hold no one's behavior against him is to choose to see. Every time I take up arms today I will remember that my sight is improved by laying them down.

Affirmation: "All power and glory lie within my harmlessness, which is of God."

Guide: My practice today will take one simple direction: **I will hurt no one in my thought or in my life.** Let me be honest in this and also in assessing its effects.

Affirmation: "Let me at least try."

Guide: God has not withheld all answers, and
if I will look within my mind, I will recognize
at least one or two small steps I can take
immediately. My need is not for mastery but
merely for the willingness to practice an instant only. A small step toward light is better
than total darkness. This day is not lost if
there is still one moment left in which to
begin again.

Affirmation: "I will not use my mind to build a case against freedom."

Guide: I will not follow up on thoughts of limitation and frailty, suffering and death. Today I will not pursue any view that would delay my return to You. For it is my quick return Home that will also release the world.

Affirmation: "Gentleness of thought is my way Home."

Guide: Do I want to take the time to justify my position, or can I lay aside shows of dignity and payments of respect as unnecessary delays? Today I will stop to ask myself if I am ready to be happy on the spot, or must I insist on handling something else first. Advancing is being very still.

Affirmation: "I will silently extend whatever I appear to lack."

Guide: Any emptiness or sense of incompletion I may feel today will indicate the gift for me to give to others. I will reach out my thoughts to fill and envelop any person who comes to mind, with a deep and satisfying gift from God's storehouse, which is my own.

Affirmation: "Give what I would have;
            see what I would be."

Guide: Within time, I must first give to receive, and see in others what I would recognize as my Self. All I have to give is an innocent vision, yet to give this is to bestow heaven itself. Today I will practice in front of God's mirror, and honor His Face in the face of every child of His.

Affirmation: "Today I will not dissociate."

Guide: Everything I see is a projection. All that I experience functions as I have set it up. My attitude alone characterizes my reality. It is not truly possible to be in touch with "my" anger because all anger is a denial of projection. Yet it is fully possible to acknowledge my deep desire to bless and set free. Today I will respond to each thing only with healing.

Affirmation: "All correction begins and ends in me."

Guide: Let me recognize the times today that I can profit from this reminder. My problem is not with another person, a circumstance, or with anything external. I do not need, nor should I work to obtain, someone's cooperation or removal or any change in the outward situation. I am the sole and proper object of my efforts to correct. My mental state will of itself extend to all those I hold in thought. That is why only my mental state needs healing.

Affirmation: "God is the power by which I rule my mind, and that power is love."

Guide: My complete release is attainable because my mind is subject to my will. It focuses where I instruct and reacts as I command. And a mind focused on God is wholly within Him. Today I choose to look for innocence and signs of gentleness, that I may begin to see What surrounds me.

Affirmation: "I will not rehearse uncertainties to come."

Guide: As best I can, I will leave myself unprepared for danger. As best I can, I will fear no evil intent and imagine no gathering storm. I will ask God what it is I need to do and, as best I can, trust every detail to His Answer.

Affirmation: "My mind is cradled in the peace of God."

Guide: Because God's love encircles it and flows softly through it, my heart beats gently. My eyes and ears are comforted by His close presence. My feet walk in the path He has prepared, and my hands hold His in love. I am His child brought safely Home.

Affirmation: "The Self that I am is God's alone."

Guide: God is not a bigger ego to which I must submit. The yearnings for good I feel deep within me are God's very Voice and my own will. There is no difference. His love is my love. His vision awakens in me the memory of my Identity. Let me treat as sacred the I that I am and see no limits or divisions to my Self. Where could the I that I am end and the I that is God begin, if All is One in Love?

Affirmation: "All is still. All is quiet. All is God."

Guide: Behind these words is the only experience that will satisfy me. Whatever troubles me, I can sing them silently and deeply and slowly in my heart. And I can see their truth within the heart of everyone I pass. You have not left me, Father. I am coming Home to You.

METAPHYSICAL
ERRANDS

MENTAL ABILITIES

Every mental ability we have can be redirected regardless of how often we may have misdirected it in the past. Memory can be used to remember the present instead of the past. Our ability to forget can be employed to release our mind from old hurts and petty lessons. Concentration can be focused on love as easily as fear. And we can use our imagination to set for ourselves a gentle path on which to walk.

Suggestion: Imagine the type day you want. Picture the kinds of exchanges you would like, the tone of your encounters, and the mental tone you want to hold to. Then remember this picture of light as you go about your day. Quickly forget to follow up on opportunities to condemn. Do not hold anyone's words against him. Concentrate on your worthiness to be happy, and release your mind from all arguments that you or anyone else deserves to lose. You did not make yourself. You were not your idea. There is Something more to you than shifting self-images. This Something makes You

worthy of your kind attention and happy concern. Look past your body and steer your mind
down only avenues that lead to life and to the
recognition that you are an inseparable part of
that which constitutes the eternal Core of all
that is going on. You do exist. And what could
possibly change that? Now is the time to face
the fact that your incalculably important mind
will not die. Return it to the peace of God so
that it can give rest to a world that has waited
too long in pain.

SALVATION WITHOUT ATTACK

Whenever we recognize that we are making a mistake, our ego will have a plan ready for our salvation: feel guilty. But that will not work. If we continue making the mistake, our ego will now tell us this proves we **are** our ego and that any effort to extricate ourselves will be futile, and therefore we should not try. It will tell us that our continuing in the mistake demonstrates that what we truly want is in competition with God's will. If that were correct, our situation would indeed be hopeless. However, it is not that we oppose God's will, but only that we misunderstand it. God's will and the will of His child are one will: satisfaction without vengeance, life without murder, and love without bounds.

Suggestion: None of your mistakes is new. They are old responses tried once again. A mistake does not add darkness; it merely continues it. It does not really matter today how long you make a mistake or how often while making it you appear to realize your error without correcting it. If you had clearly recognized the nature of your mistake even once, you would have already stopped. All that is important is whether you are now ready to make a gentle effort on your own behalf. Whenever you feel strong enough, lay aside the evidence of your guilt and of the hopelessness of your condition, and quietly let all fear pass from your mind. Be calm a moment, and then remember that God could not be mistaken in what He sees in you. You are His. You are not owned by an ego. End your period of rest by trying awhile to feel the way you imagine it would feel to be God's very own child. If you succeed in having this sense of peace, even for an instant, you will recognize that what made the mistake was never part of you.

AN INDIRECT APPROACH

Belief is made by wish.

Suggestion: Rather than attempt a direct release of your present beliefs about this room, that rug, those people, there may be times when it would be helpful to adopt a gradual approach. Begin by asking yourself what would you like to believe about this chair, that phone call, the way the day is going, or whatever you find your attention has turned to. Imagine it the way you would like to see it. In this way you are working directly with how you desire to see and feel and not arguing with yourself about "how things really are." Now it does not matter that you think you are unable to see a gentle light within this person, for you will begin by trying to imagine that you can. This would be dishonest if you were a victim of the world you see. But you are not. If you see another's innocence, he will lead you to yours. If you see him as shameful or self-betraying, he will function only as your guide to pain. Either perception is your choice. However, one is based on fact; the other on a misinterpretation, and that is why it is not dishonest to use an indirect approach if your purpose is to walk around mental confusion. Close your eyes and ask yourself what you would wish to see if you could, and how you would feel on seeing it. Remind yourself of the beauty God has placed within every living thing, and then take one person as your subject and try to recall what true loveliness is like. That memory is still within you.

FORGIVING

Guided Meditation

Step 1: Think of someone you are angry with. Anyone you have found difficult at times or who brings to mind a fearful thought will be an adequate subject. Take a moment or two to picture this person in detail. How he stands. How he dresses. How he has behaved toward you and others. Remember anything about his body or mannerisms you do not like. Also include whatever features you consider special.

Step 2: Recall a moment when you or someone else was thoughtful or gentle. The incident does not have to involve the person in Step 1. Just think of a time when any adult, child, or animal extended its love to another. And notice the soft light and sense of relaxation that comes into your mind with this thought. Using the touch you would use to communicate your tenderness and love, shape this light into a garment. And gently place this garment of light over the person in Step 1. Allow yourself a minute or so to see the soft glow that now envelops him.

Step 3:   As you continue to watch, see standing behind him a brilliant figure of light. This is the Christ, who comes to heal and forgive. Please watch as He walks into this person you did not love without limit. Now not only the light of your love covers him, but the Light of God fills him entirely, and he becomes very still within God's peace as he feels the release within your mind, and in his own.

THE GENTLE REALITY

Guided Meditation: You have before you a little box. It contains a new set of eyes made purely of love. You screw out your present set and screw in the new one. For just a moment you leave your eyelids closed and think of all the distressing images your old eyes brought to you. Now you open and then quickly close your new eyes. The light of the world you just saw was very bright indeed. You wish to look more fully on such a lovely place, and so you slowly open your eyes again, and allow all good things to come into view.

Mantra:
Let all voices but Love's be still in me.
Let all visions but Christ's Face be unseen.
Now I feel only the oneness of One
No memory remains but God my Self
There can be nothing now but what I am
The truth is true; I am all that I am, forever.

TIME HAS ENDED

Guided Meditation: You are presently standing at the end of time looking back. You have merely picked out a particular series of events and have focused your thought upon them. It all seems very real indeed, and the windings of the plot you are involved in appear demanding and most important. But now there comes a stillness over you, as if some dear Friend is gently placing his hand upon your brow. Softly he speaks this reminder: "You have only drawn an old nightmare into your mind. Nothing more. Relax your mental hold on it and let this scene of disaster return to the dust of time." You watch the sad and frantic tale you called your life recede. It fades as it returns to time, and dissolves completely from your mind. Now you are beside your God. A creation of pure joy held safely in His Love. Your mind is no longer trapped inside a dying body. You are free.

JESUS

Guided Meditation: Turn very specifically to Jesus and ask him direct questions. Do not tell him the form that his answer must take. Leave that to him. Simply consult him as **your** elder brother, who loves you, and knows your way home. What do you have to lose by acknowledging an experience greater than yours? He has said there is nothing about him you cannot attain. Is it truly less idolatrous to call a spiritual advisor on the phone or to read a book of printed truths than it is to consult one who has traveled every step of the road before you? Perhaps you feel foolish talking to someone you think is dead or possibly never was? Yet is it not clear that there is a specific wisdom which transcends the "lessons" of our very short personal history? What could you suffer by trusting in what you have always professed to believe: that time and death have not changed reality? All that our body perceives is not all there is. For one free moment, gently lay aside your arguments and your fears of appearing ridiculous and **see** if there is not Someone who waits to bless and guide you.

MASTERY AND EFFORT

There is a useful distinction to be made between mastery and effort. Our ego (there is really only one ego or mental mistake even though we each make it in a different way) will frequently point out that we have not mastered forgiveness. This is true but irrelevant since our part is only to make the effort to forgive. Any interest in external results comes from the ego.

Suggestion: The next time you feel defeated or confused, make the effort to think a thought with some degree of love in it. Any thought will do. For example, picture a gentle exchange between you and a friend. Or picture the opposing sides in a current world conflict throwing down their weapons and running to embrace those they had mistaken as their enemy. See the tears of happiness simple forgiveness brings. If you would rather, make your effort this way: Assume a relaxed position, close your eyes, and silently and very slowly repeat the name of God. As you do so, focus your mind on the Experience behind the word, and allow your mind to be drawn into that Experience. If you prefer mental

81

stillness to images or words, then let your effort take that direction. Every religious, mystical, therapeutic, or philosophical system in the world entails concentration in some form, so do not throw out the one aspect of effort that can be of genuine use to you, under the mistaken assumption that to remain mentally scattered is a form of acceptance. Make your effort in the way you wish for as long as there is no distress, then go about your day without looking back to judge the results. When you feel ready, try again. Each attempt you make will cause another desirable shift in the direction of your mind. And sooner than you think you will complete your goal of turning it right-side-up.

THE ONE REMINDER

There is one reminder we cannot make too often: **"I am not alone."** There is Someone with us even now. In **this** place and time and situation. That is why we never need do something else first. Not even one thought must be first correct by ourselves. In fact, we can do nothing by ourselves. And our ego is merely our belief that we can.

ADDRESSING THOUGHT

We need only address God in our mind. There is really nothing else that has to be pictured or spoken to. The past need not be reactivated, or figures from old or recent scenes readdressed in sharper terms. It will not make us safer to fantasize the future and then lay plans to prevent what we have fantasized. Each insight we receive from God does not have to be mentally repeated to an imagined someone we think needs to hear it more than we do.

Suggestion: Within the quietness of your thought, you can safely talk to God, and God alone. Any scene you call to mind that serves to denounce your motives will merely waste your time. It will frighten you and appear to weaken you because of the "laws" it affirms. Whenever you notice this "idle thinking," gently return your mind to something that matters. It is indeed possible to save yourself time. All things are beneficial, yet you can do something, one thing at least, to increase their beneficial effect for you: You can address no one but God within your mind. Speak to Him in your deep and silent heart, where the hush of His holiness enfolds you in peace.

FEAR OF UNITY

Why do we resist loving certain people? Is it not because we have judged someone and do not want to unite with what we believe is a distasteful reality? If his character were as we believe it to be, our resistance to him would be reasonable and correct. The ego does suspect that love joins completely with everything it sees, but it does not suspect that everything love sees is desirable and only what love sees is real.

Suggestion: In the presence of this person you dislike, either thought of or before you now, gently release yourself from your defensiveness. Become harmless before him. Become as blameless as rain falling on grass. Slowly lay down your armor and breathe away your piercing screams of fear. Quiet all thoughts of objection, however mild or great. Then open as a flower to the sun: without effort and without thought. As all defenses fall away, you will see plainly that your fears were groundless. Only your judgments frightened you, not this gentle child of God who yearns only for what you yearn: to be seen as innocent in all he truly wants.

PLEASANT EFFORT

If you feel discouraged about your progress, if you want to take the next step and yet the thought of even taking the first step tires or saddens you, know that you are mistaken about what is expected of you. Effort is to be used only as a means of letting go of effort. You simply make the effort to remember that you need do nothing. Yes, you are to be firm with yourself, but only to the end of staying mentally clear that you do not know your way home, that you do not even know the next step to be taken, and that your strength can only come in putting yourself completely back into the arms of the One who carries you. The biggest hindrance to our spiritual progress is our suspicion that we are being asked to figure something out and do something other than rest in peace. Behind these fears is an assumption that the rules whereby one advances demand a sacrifice, e.g., "nothing worth having comes easy." So we think we are being asked to do a thing that will be unpleasant or tedious. But this will never be so. The rules of advancement call for the very opposite: rest, quiet contentment, and freedom.

Suggestion: It is not ever possible that you could truly want to do something that would constitute a retreat from your heart's goal. If ever you think that, you have merely misunderstood where your treasure lies. When you find that you are irritated or dejected, or when there is even the slightest sense that you are fighting yourself: do nothing. Doing nothing is all you ever need do. But you do need to do that much. Admit how little you know and then mentally step aside. Wait for Him to move. We are like a child, and He is like a shining train that will take us into a land of unexpected beauty and wonder. Our part is merely to allow ourselves to be carried along.

PREOCCUPATIONS

Dwell not on the distressing, the complicated, and the doubtful. Dwell not on things of smallness: little hurts and petty accomplishments. Dwell instead on some kindness given, on some sign of thoughtfulness. Dwell on clarity, simplicity, and trust. You are one. Dwell only on what can be extended and shared so that your mind may remain one. One in peace and love. One in its healing vision. Quickly forgive another his mistakes. Do not leave your mind at war. Look instantly beyond the little interferences, no matter what their form, so you may continue to hear a single Voice and see a single Self. Waking up is not difficult provided you do not let your mind drift back into concerns of any sort. Look at what makes you happy to see. Try, at least. Only a single vision can help and heal. One divided has already become part of the problem it beholds. Oneness, simplicity, and kindliness are a Thought that is highly practical and effective. But choose it because it is true. Keep your interpretations fresh and still by interesting yourself in the points of light around you. All you attempt is to see that they do in fact exist. Allow this recognition to come softly into your single mind. A single vision, carried everywhere you go, is heaven.

TOUCHSTONES

What does your mind return to for safety? What is its place of rest, the "reality" it grounds itself in whenever it feels hassled or bleak? Is it the time of day? Do you look at your watch? Is it some activity you have planned for this evening? Or some broader consummation or life victory you hope for? Or perhaps you "rest" in the thought of what "you" contain, your influence or appearance, your location or your name. Or is it some thought of what you have accumulated: property or savings or a "fine" family or "good" friends? Does your mind return to some external such as these for a little reassurance that the present turmoil really does not matter? If so, you have not yet changed your reason for being here. Yet you can, now, if you wish. You already know that the little platforms on which you attempt to rest, whatever they may be, will eventually collapse. Because they always have. And if now you frantically build your health, or desperately you hold to your loved ones, or quite deliberately you secure your reputation, it is only a matter of time before you see once again how frail and meaningless were these defenses. But you need not continue in this manner. Put your weight on something that will bear it. You will recognize what you are relying on by what your mind keeps returning to for reassurance. If it is God, your increasing peace and confidence are assured. If it is a single thought of beauty, you have picked wisely, and you have indeed chosen for the future and not just for a few fleeting moments. Peace is not external. But it **is** internal. Like a pond ruffled by a passing wind, merely return again to peace. Make peace your home, your touchstone, your shelter, and your goal. No matter how often you stumble, make your single response to wait in stillness for your God.

VAGUE GUILT

It is not possible to know the answer and yet not
apply it. If you have a vague feeling that you
know what you should be doing, but are not doing it, you are mistaken. Your ego does not
know anything, but it thinks it does. It therefore
wants you to feel guilty for not applying its
answer. But it has no answer.

Suggestion: Address directly your suspicion
that you know the way out. Ask yourself what
specifically you are supposed to be doing. If
what you now hear is still coming from your
ego, you will not be able to complete what you
think you should, no matter what it is. Now turn
to God. Do not prepare yourself first. Honestly
admit that you do not possess "good" judgment
and that you need help. Yesterday's lesson will
not work today. Turn to God because of your
honest recognition that you are not clear how to
respond to this, and then wait in peace for the
answer. Drop all your demands and your definition of the situation. You cannot define the
situation you think you are in without believing
you know what the problem is that needs solv-

ing, and you cannot believe in a problem without feeling guilty for not applying the answer, even though you do not have one. The answer will come, but not from the direction your ego thinks. Simply wait, and in the meantime do not judge anything. Your part is merely to resign as your own analyst. It is a small part but absolutely essential to your freedom.

INNOCENCE

There is no fear greater than the fear of being happy. There is no reluctance more deeply seated than the unwillingness to see all faults and sins as simply mistakes. Who could honestly denounce another if it was admitted that all he had done was make a mistake? Instead, the other is seen as selfish and internally dark, a thing unworthy of life, to be attacked and weakened. To have any hope of happiness, we must first recognize those times we are afraid of the innocence of others. They are the same moments as when we ourselves resist feeling gentle and free. We mistakenly believe that our sense of self-worth comes from how we compare to others, and that to see them as innocent would reflect badly on us. So we remain hard and exacting in order not to allow any evidence of guilt to go unnoticed. But our fear of the sinlessness of what God has created also leaves no possibility of recognizing our own inherent worthiness. Let us therefore practice genuine self-interest. Let us renounce anxiety and try in its place an experiment in kindness.

BEAUTIFUL BALLOON

Guided Meditation: There are two perceptions of this world: one dark, the other bright; one heavy and bleak and desperate, the other abounding in life and sparkling with love and peace. One is certainly hell, the other heaven. You have seen the world both ways, although your memory of the latter vision may seem distant to you now. Rest a moment in peace, and then imagine your mind as a beautiful and buoyant balloon. Its nature is to soar in freedom and enter Heaven effortlessly. But now it is chained to a world that is old and tired, a place where all things have grown weary with hollow victories and inevitable endings. Today it is within your power to release it and let it fly to its natural Home. It will carry you fully within it wherever it goes, for it is your mind. The chains that hold you to a barren world are all the separate things you think meaningful, each high as well as the lows. If it has some special meaning for you, it binds you to this perception. Fear something no longer, and that chain is broken. Withdraw your longing from another, and another tie is released. What binds you comes in many forms and names, and they vary more or less with each person: something owned or wanted, influence sought or lost, an imagined slight or one given, great personal tragedy that lends an aura of awe, adornments, regimes of health or beauty, past lives as proof of attainment, special gifts and powers. Whatever seems to make your staying here a little longer enticing in any way anchors you to this world, until that time you are willing to take a more honest look at just what it is you cherish. Take that time now. Review the anchors and the chains. Do not overlook your list of personal attributes as well as your imagined failings. Then lightly toss each of these weights from off your mind, until, clean and free, you can leave the old world behind, not as something you dislike, but as a place that no longer has any meaning for you at all. And soar like a beautiful balloon into the light of a new and rapturous world, which is your Life and your right.

MENTAL PROJECTS

DECISIONS

When our purpose is clear, there is no question what to do. Ultimately, we cannot make a mistake, for God has provided a Purpose to all we have done even though our motives may have been insincere at the time. Love uses all to bless all.

Our progress is seen not in what we do but in what we perceive our goal to be. Either we assign our ego's objective or God's purpose, and that is determined by what we choose to consult within us at the time each decision is made. It is impossible not to consult something. If we think that our experience is our guide, we will not believe that the still and present urgings of Love direct us.

God's purpose cannot be surmised or rationalized. It must be seen. We cannot merely second-guess because that is a form of avoidance and serves only to strengthen our belief that goodness is disguised and that what is meant to help us can be sent to us in the form of a curse. This of course is nonsense and is not a truly helpful way of looking at anything. God is fair and Truth is unequivocal.

Asking for guidance from our deep core of peace will facilitate our recognition of the loving consequence of all we do. Asking, however, is not what establishes a beneficial result. Blessing is our inheritance from God and is therefore our right. It cannot be negated, but it can most certainly be overlooked. Turning every decision over to God protects our mind from a loveless view.

A question that often arises is, "If all things are beneficial, and if the past contains no mistakes, what is the point in asking for guidance? Won't the results be the same?" Yes. But not our experience of the results. How we see the world constitutes the world we see. The love content of our perception will determine how we will characterize our relationships, our health, and our apparent destiny. It will make life a living heaven or hell for us and for those we keep in mind.

What we turn to for counsel will not cause the future, but it will cause our experience of it. In this respect, our happiness comes from accepting God's direction and losing interest in all ego suggestions and merely personal interests. "Everything the ego tells you that you need will hurt you," says **A Course in Miracles**.

Since we operate most of the time as if the future course of our lives were up to us alone, it is helpful in freeing the mind from fear to ask for guidance in all decisions concerning the future. Begin with those decisions you recognize and do not judge their importance. Ask what you are to do. The answer will come quickly. If it does not, wait happily until you feel the need to ask again.

A good general rule is to not ask what to do until the time for the decision has come. To ask God prematurely is merely to request that He relieve your anxiety, and the answer you receive may do no more than that. It will not necessarily relate to the guidance you will receive later. A second general rule is to never reconsider unless it appears that by your continuing in that decision someone is being hurt.

It is possible for us to so weaken our ability to hear that the answer will seem to come and go or will only be heard after we have asked more than once. But this is not necessary and merely adds uncertainty to the process. When you act on the answer you hear, it is the right answer, and your ability to hear clearly and quickly grows as a consequence.

The third guideline is a general observation of the manner in which guidance often comes to mind. It is unlikely that you will be given broad instructions about drastic changes in your life situation. It is much more likely that you will be told each step at the time it is to be taken. It is therefore helpful to remind yourself frequently that you do not know what anything you have been told is leading to. Certainly there is no merely personal goal you could think of that would throw light on the Purpose behind your inner instructions. And never is what you are told to do designed to point up your guilt or un- worthiness. Be content to take each small step as it is given you, knowing the time will surely come when you will look back and see a mean- ing more vast and beautiful than anything you have ever imagined.

The apparent need to decide is actually a mo- ment of internal conflict. The mind pauses in uncertainty. Asking for guidance is a safe way to acknowledge your Source and to return your mind to peace. However, when you are exper- iencing no hesitation in what you do, it is not necessary to ask about every detail. When you feel carried along, and all those around you are comfortable, there is no need to ask God for ad- vice. Simply continue to move in love and in confidence.

Whenever feasible, turn your moments of ask- ing into moments of quiet listening. There is no question about what to do, and this is the only lesson we are actually learning. Our will and the will of God are in fundamental agreement. Only the ego is undecided. Only it experiences the need to question. Our purpose is to step quietly around doubt and confusion and proceed in peace. If we can accomplish this through questionless listening and pure thanks, we are better off than if we believe the advice we received was the entire Answer. So whenever circumstances allow, relinquish your assessment of the problem, drop all questions and demands, and turn directly to God. All you need say or do will be answered in His peace.

We do not make the course of future events, for to do that would render God's Plan meaningless. We could not misplace ourselves without altering the activities of everyone we encountered. If the universe contained a single mistake, it would affect its perfect functioning throughout. The altering of reality is not a part of free will, and yet the ego will counsel that by admitting our fallibility we remain humble. But is it humble to claim the capacity to change Truth?

We do not personally stand at the point of control but at the point of choice between two interpretations. We do not choose between a thousand different futures, but we do decide how we will characterize our part in the interchange of love between God's children. We are not in control of external events because only by defining ourselves as something small and weak could we believe that anything was external. As a body, everything comes to us as a surprise. Only the degree of the surprise varies. We

try to exert ourselves; we attempt to take our little lives into our own hands and to make others
behave, but very quickly any sense of our having made advances in this direction is shattered.

Within Love's perception there is clearly
another Maker of this world. All mistakes are
translated by It into precise steps toward
freedom. We cannot do anything that has not
been anticipated and turned into a benefit for us
and for all the world. But this must be seen
before it will be recognized as true within our
experience. On the level of divine interpretation,
all that is true in Heaven is true on earth. And
this **can** be seen as the way things actually
operate now and here. In Heaven there is no
need for decisions because All has been given
by God to His creation, and so it will be forever.

We do not need to concern ourselves with
how we can have more, but we do need to see
that we have everything. A future would be required only to provide us with what we presently
lack. But what could possibly be added to
everything? Our path is a mental shift from a
dream of needs to a reality of wholeness and
love.

Within this world, we are merely reviewing
what has already happened. We are taking a last
look at an old and hopeless dream. A review
does not call for choices between events but for
a reinterpretation of the whole. All that occurs

in a dream is the same. And our only real choice is to continue dreaming or to awake. In the beginning, Adam fell asleep. There is no record of his having awakened **because** he has not yet done so. He dreams even now of disrupting God's reality and of punishing himself to prove the actuality of this "sin." It is only a dream. God comes now to wake us. It is a gentle awakening because all we thought we did to Him had no effect. He remains forever Love. And you are the child He loves.

A thousand times today we will be presented with the opportunity to awake. Seeing that this opportunity always exists, the advanced student no longer concerns himself with the future. His interest is in this instant alone. He is content for the events imagined by his ego to unfold as they will, for he recognizes that whatever direction they take they cannot affect his reality or the reality of all his brothers and sisters. Instead, he turns from every aspect of self-deception and disengages his mind from choices that are all the same. He chooses God. He chooses straightforward love, immediate helpfulness, and true charity. His only questions are: Am I willing to fulfill the function Love has given me? Am I willing to forgive all my hallucinations and return to His peace? Am I willing to be happy and free for one eternal instant, and through my holy mind, bring rest to all the world?

IDLE THOUGHTS

The body, in all its many activities, does not require the cooperation of the mind. The mind can heal the body, but the body, being an effect of the mind, cannot of itself call to the mind, change it, diminish it, or extinguish it.

Although your ego will claim you must "think about" what you are doing, this is not actually necessary. It is a substitute for concentration that is merely the ego's ploy to remove your mind from your control, or at least to make you think you have. Your ego suggests that perhaps you would like to keep your mind in love, but alas, there is a worldly task before you that requires worldly thought.

All things will fall more easily into place if your mind is not conflicted about what you are doing; for example, if you are not wishing you were someplace else or if you are not seeing what you are doing as proof of your sinfulness. Whenever you are inwardly happy, you will not be distracted. And your body will function efficiently. A highly active mind **is** distracted, whereas internal comfort allows the mind to concentrate naturally.

After you have had a quiet moment with God,

your ego may suggest there is now something practical you must do and that all of this spiritual stuff must be laid aside so you can keep your mind on what you are about to engage in. If you were to then rest your mind fully on the activity before you, this would indeed be a pure and perfect form of meditation. Yet, if you will observe closely, you will see that as your body undertakes the activity, your mind is not now focused on what you are doing, but is standing back and commenting on it. It frequently drifts off to think about something not even indirectly related to the task. It aimlessly passes from one subject to another, apparently at random.

The terms "idle thinking," "projection," "mental miscreation," "dissociation," and "loveless thinking," are interchangeable. They only emphasize different aspects of the same mistake. What, then, is "idle thought"? It is thought that appears to be idle or neutral but is not. It is any thought we believe remains within the head and does not go forth to make the world we see. A "private" thought that carries no consequences. A thought that changes nothing, affects no one, and therefore is undeserving of our attention or remedy.

This "idle thinking" is in fact a very deliberate form of repair and maintenance undertaken by the ego. It systematically mends all the fences that were weakened during your moment of peace. It is anything but a neutral activity, for it reinforces the thought system on which your entire perceptual world rests. It is not harmless, because all forms of pain flow either directly or indirectly from this single mental activity.

The difference between "fantasizing," "dreaming," "perceiving," and what usually passes for just plain "thinking" are the apparent length and intensity of the fantasies involved. These differences are imposed in retrospect. All mental activity is the same except what is within the Mind of God. The kind of "thinking" we are most familiar with is composed of very short fantasies about the past or future. Words are indeed "heard," but words of themselves have no meaning without a mental referent or impression. "Thinking," in whatever form taken, is an attempt to rehearse or rewrite, to plan or reactivate. It overlooks now and deals with an imaginary time that is finished or is yet to be. Very little real thought is contained in this process, because thought is a calm seeing and is accompanied by a pure delight with the whole contents of the mind. Real thought is love.

True thoughtfulness is never off on some hopeless search, as all seeking for what one does not presently have must be. It is an act of present discovering and present finding. It is simple acknowledgment of what one truly and deeply possesses. It is gratitude, the only mental activity that joins with God.

The beginning step in freeing the mind from its useless wanderings is stillness. Stillness may be associated with physical quietness, but the effort must be made to carry mental calmness and peace into every situation the body enters or else a severe limitation on one's happiness has been left in place.

Far more moments than one may recognize at first have already been provided during which it will be feasible to pause and speak to God. The first broadening of the instant of stillness may therefore be the willingness to make use of these periods of rest, the opportunities for which will appear to multiply as they are utilized. Nor is it a mistake to deliberately plan these moments into one's daily schedule. As long as we believe in planning, we **will** exercise that belief, and it will benefit us more to exercise it lovingly instead of fearfully.

As you sincerely try to bring goodwill into every activity, the means whereby this can be accomplished will be provided. A **search** for means is merely a delaying tactic of the ego. Your honest desire to be in love and of love is all you need. It is not possible for you to want an increase in mental freedom without being shown precisely how to obtain it.

"Ask and you shall receive" is an instruction

for successful prayer that points to our heart, not to the Heart of God. Discover what you truly desire and you will have it, for God unfailingly gives. But when we are afraid to be free of all problems, God will not do anything to increase our fear. Therefore, "be not afraid." Search gently within your heart to find what you honestly want. Seeing what you want, you will no longer be afraid.

As was stated before, you do not have to "think about" what you are doing, only seek peace in what you are doing. You do not have to use words in order to think; however, at the outset, words can often be useful in directing thought. A single focus is used as a replacement for the hundreds of conflicting focuses your ego will offer you. The time will come when you will be able to leave your mind unguarded and it will no longer project or dissociate. Yet it is clear that there are very few who have reached this level of learning. I can assure you that I have not. Nor do I know anyone personally who has. So I merely offer you the words that have helped me begin to relinquish the need for words.

First, we only say the truth. We accept it intellectually. Then, we begin to suspect the truth may in fact be true because of the evidence for it we are starting to see in our experience. Later, we grow in fondness and in trust of the truth.

And finally, we recognize that we ourselves are true.

Because all minds are joined, everything in our environment does the same thing at the same time. If I defend my ego, all the egos around me defend themselves at the same instant. If I feel defensive while physically by myself, the egos that people my thought will appear to be defensive within my fantasies. And if I am dreaming, the figures in my dream will protect themselves, each against the other. Only the personal manifestations that the defensiveness takes will contrast. Each ego will defend itself in its own way, and these **forms** of acting out may differ widely, but at the center of each will be a knot of fear. Viewed in this way, another's behavior, whether fantasized, dreamed, or seen physically, acts as a helpful alarm that warns us that we are hurting ourselves by continuing to sustain our present attitude. And this attitude is manufactured by so-called idle thoughts.

Although a little effort is needed to keep the mind from spinning tales of limitation and attack, it is a restful effort and a much more enjoyable use of the mind than the ego's version of "letting go" or "giving up." When the mind drifts off into conflict, the pressure can become enormous and the distress quite noticeable. Now comes the alternative of a little peace and quiet. Turn your thoughts to God and partake of His pleasant imagery and healing considerations. There is no limit to the number and variety of thoughts you can think that contain love. Direct thought to this single purpose, and every point in consciousness will relax. Nor will the world itself remain unaffected by your gentle choice.

DREAMS

If this is a dream, don't you want to wake up?
Maybe you are afraid that reality is not an improvement on your present experience. Possibly
you wish to wait a little longer to see how a
special person or a certain course of events will
turn out. Or is it that you are afraid of losing the
little you have and perhaps even your identity?

What are you if you are not a body? Where
are you if you are not confined to this particular
time and place? Perhaps these questions
frighten you.

If this book is correct in its assumptions,
everything that is being discussed here can
already be found reflected in your experience.
The question it attempts to raise is only whether
you wish to continue experiencing everything
you now experience, or can you safely release
yourself from certain thoughts and "realities."

It is clear that whatever we think is real will
be reflected outwardly in what we see. Yet when
different "realities" are observed to conflict and
refute each other, a choice will be made between these contrasting sets of evidence
because they point to opposite conclusions. A
good example of this is in the question of what

we are at our core. What do we feel most deeply—a desire to heal or one to destroy? If the kingdom of God is truly within us, then that same position is not occupied by a powerful evil. To think that light and darkness are at the same point is to defer thinking altogether. And yet our present way of seeing others is highly conflicted. We first see darkness and then light, light and then darkness, as the basic motivating urge within those we encounter. The problem is not in their motivation but in our vacillating perception.

As has been stated several times in this book, for everything we see there are two interpretations. These windows of perception appear to open onto opposite worlds. Looked at fearfully, a person will appear to be motivated quite differently than he is when looked at with love. Because the world we see reflects only our choice of what we want to be real, there is no external world. Truth is not separate from us. When we finally awake there will be no need for perception because nothing will be separate and at a distance. In the meantime, the world we see is the best of teaching devices because it instantly reflects back to us a picture of where we want to be. When all things are seen as good and kind and lovely, we will be willing, and therefore ready, to wake to a Reality that is entirely Love.

The question, "Am I ready to enter Heaven?"

is therefore answered by a second question. "Do I see only Heaven reflected everywhere I look? For what I see is what I want."

Our dreams at night are excellent illustrations of how the mind can create an entire world and then forget the part it has played. The project proposed here is simply for you to practice transferring your knowledge of the dynamics of perception to new areas of experience. You will take what is clear in one part of your life—what happens when you dream at night—and apply it to those times when you do not distinguish clearly between truth and illusion. In order to do this, you must allow yourself to practice an assumption that you may disagree with intellectually. You are not asked to believe this working premise, but you are requested to test it for yourself.

The waking dream and the sleeping dream, although differing at times in the "laws" they represent, are equally dream states. All that is seen by the body's eyes, whether it is by the body that moves about in a dream or by the one that arises after a night's sleep, is a projection. Not a projection by the body, but a projection of the mind.

This is not a difficult point to grasp because you already recognize that it is true of your dreams at night. During sleep your mind pictures itself as a body that may be similar or dissimilar from the body that lies in bed. This dream-body, or body within the dream, does not think. The dreamer thinks for it. While we are dreaming we believe that our mind is contained wholly within a particular figure that we have identified with in the dream, but neither that figure nor any part of its anatomy is doing the thinking.

All the figures in a dream appear to think, but it is still the dreamer, who lies asleep, who thinks for them. You, as God's child, are merely asleep in Him. You dream that you are a body. Yet you are pure mind. You dream you are attacked by other bodies. Yet these too are only pictures in your mind. To love all these parts of your mind is to take the first step toward awaking in God.

If, then, we form our waking experience in the same way we do our dreams, what else can be said to be true of both, and what lessons can be learned? Here are just a few:

1. Although all perception is a dream, there are two kinds of dream activity. Who has not heard God speak to him in a dream, or at least felt for an instant the deep peace of Love? One kind of dreaming reflects what is true of our relationship to God, the other kind refutes fairness and everything that is eternal. Our present work is to practice the first step of dreaming only the Christ-dream or dream of forgiveness.

The second step, that of awaking in God, cannot be taken until the first is completed. And everyone must complete it.

Within our minds is at least the suspicion that all we do is for purely personal interests, that we have at one time or another misused all our friends and have wasted our time and talents on small and unworthy pursuits. This suspicion about our basic motivation operates as an underlying tone to all we think and do. Consequently, a sense of guilt is never entirely absent. No matter what we attempt, we cannot experience one unequivocal instant of release. But is this entirely true?

As in dreams, there have been at least a few instances of release within everyone's life. At times they can become so dim in his memory that he may wonder whether they occurred at all. Did he deceive himself in this as he has in so many other things? They did occur most certainly. In fact, they are the only things reflecting reality that have.

These moments of pure seeing have certain characteristics that distinguish them from the way of perceiving with which we are most familiar. Within their light the past and future become unthinkable, so absorbed are we in the beauty that surrounds us. Nowhere do we see a thing we do not like. Our way Home is certain now, and we are content to leave all things in

His hands. Our mind stays fixed on nothing but instead moves freely about from one scene of joy to another. The "evidence" for guilt simply cannot enter our awareness because we are wholly fair and generous.

By contrast, a loveless perception is the movie of a temper tantrum. Everything seen holds something we do not like, and the only question is whether to reject it now or later. Nothing is left unjudged. Innocence is a matter of degree, and peace is merely the thought that someone suffers more than we. Since this type of dream activity consists wholly of comparisons, everything is seen at odds with everything else, and friends are only those with whom we feel the least competitive at the moment.

Our present experience is clearly a mixture of both a fearless perception and one that is fear dominated. Our problem now is that we become confused as to which has value. We love a little and attack a little, and no real progress is made.

But aren't you already noticing that the differences in texture, shape, quantity, and degree within the world of form begin to diminish in importance as true beauty is seen? Haven't there already been moments when **every** detail has been lovely, not just a fleeting few? When the heart is gentle and compassionate, another's body is no longer an adequate source of information about his true motive and character. Distance becomes less relevant to communication. Even death can fade as a block to the awareness of another's presence. And Something within this universal undoing of limitations quietly informs us that nothing happens without our permission. Just as in a dream. This new recognition of our complete responsibility does not point to our guilt. It sets us free. As it does when a dreamer becomes aware of his responsibility for a dream. He sees he is innocent because he has not changed the nature of reality and **can** change the nature of the dream.

2. Unless what has happened in a dream is thought to indicate a fact about physical "reality" (an assumption made in various systems of dream interpretation), anything that is seen as merely a dream is easily and quickly dismissed. Who continues to argue with a figure in a dream once he has awakened? And who, having seen that the direction of events was merely dreamed, continues to plan against it? In short, no one reacts to what he recognizes to be mere illusion.

Applying this fact to our daily life, we realize that nothing needs to be forgiven in ourselves or others, but that its unreality does need to be acknowledged. "You can forgive but you can't forget," becomes, "You can only forgive by forgetting." A thing is forgotten when it is recognized as insignificant. Any form that fear takes is not important when seen in the light of Love.

3. How the mind imagines itself as something it is not is also clearly seen in dreams. Not only is a body required—something to see and hear with—but other bodies are also needed to react to it and "prove" through independent witnesses that it is indeed a thing set apart.

As children, many of us had imaginary playmates. Here again is a thing set up in thought to act as if it has a separate mind and will. And for as long as we saw a benefit in its remaining, it indeed appeared to act independently of us. Any attempt we made to get rid of it would merely have strengthened its sense of reality within us because there was no real playmate to get rid of. Only our loss of interest in the purpose it served made it disappear. For it was our mind alone that sustained it.

An ego is very similar to an imaginary playmate. It is an imaginary identity. And, like any other hallucination, it is merely strengthened when confronted directly. That is why "Do not fight yourself" is the first rule of safety. What you are fighting is your imaginary identity. Merely cut off its source of power and the ego fades. And its source is always our interest in the purpose it serves. When we are no longer interested in being separate, in being special, or set apart in any way, but are fully occupied with love and desirous of uniting with everything around us, we will have no purpose for an ego, and so there will be none in our experience.

4. All misery is in one spot. Although there are thousands of things going on in a dream, there is only one dream. Whatever cannot learn this is also in the dream. Whatever is depressed, cruel, sad, defeated, in pain, fearful, arrogant, or deceived is in a dream, because our imaginary identity is contained wholly within the part of our mind that hallucinates, just as it was when we slept last night. That is why the Answer is so simple. Wake up. But how? Decide for any component of the waking state—forgiveness, grace, happiness, rest, honesty, fairness, now, gentleness, love, stillness—and, to that degree, we release the dreaming part of our mind from its dream and from all the problems it contains. That part of our mind is then free to continue its return to peace.

If you attempt to focus on something and consider it apart from its context, and then try to change it, you may succeed in eliminating that **form** of pain, but you will still be in pain. If while you were dreaming that the devil was chasing you, someone gently whispered, "It is time to get up," you would merely remain asleep if you insisted on first escaping the devil. Do not say, "I must first change this about myself," because whatever struggles is not part of you. Instead, say, "I need only turn from murder, whatever form it takes, and wake to my Self, the Christ, the Identity I have in common with God."

5. The title of one of my books, **There Is a Place Where You Are Not Alone**, came in part from my recognition that I, like every dreamer, am alone in my dream. When I awake from sleep I understand that all those who appeared to surround me in the dream were neither animate nor inanimate; they were simply imagined. My mind had divided itself into figures, and I had actually conversed with no one separate from myself. The people in my dream had served the purpose of convincing me that what was external functioned independently of my wish and that I was therefore not responsible for the loveless behavior of others, for their sins, or their pains. For in my dream I had thought from inside a head, and lived inside a body, and had peered out through eyes at strange and unasked for events. Nothing was my responsibility except my own protection. I was the sole provider of my happiness, and whatever I did in this respect was innocent in comparison to what was occurring around me.

Yet all of that was an illusion of the dream. I was alone in my private fantasy. There is, however, a place where we are not alone, where whatever is seen reflects truth accurately because it is not viewed as separate from us. In the experience of God, nothing but life can be touched. There are no bodies with sightless eyes, nor desperate minds caged inside skulls. Life does not submit to dying flesh, and "success" is not reserved for the fortunate and the few. Each and all is known as One in the embrace of joy. There is suspicion no longer because nothing can be hidden in Love.

Of this we have but glimpses as yet. But those gentle liftings of the shroud of fear do come, and they reveal a world alive with contentment and brilliant with caring. Every time we choose simple peace in place of any aspect of a nightmare, we wake more certainly and live more fully. In God we are not alone.

6. If one were to read superficially what has been said so far about dreams, one might think this approach could result in callous treatment of other people. After all, they are just figures in a dream. If only this half-truth were seen, the outcome would indeed be lacking in kindness. The sole purpose of recognizing what part of our experience is illusion is to see more clearly and respond more fully to the part that has true value. If we accord attack and love equal value, we are not in position to confer a real blessing because we unwittingly withdraw it the moment we extend it. And this type of conflicted

message does characterize what passes for communication between most people. We believe we can correct another without making him unhappy. This confusion arises from an improper distinction between dreaming and loving.

It is only the dream aspect of other people that can be safely neglected. Whatever is seen with love is not an ego dream. It is a reflection of reality, and once it is seen it cannot possibly be neglected.

We wake up **by** loving other people because only love sees Love without distortion. Coolness and arrogance are not vision. A reflection of Love **can** be seen in any aspect of the dream because what is true is never entirely absent from our mind. The whole content of our mind is present in our perceptual world, but it is not always recognized.

Imperfect glass can appear to distort a landscape that is viewed through it. But the glass does not actually change any part of the landscape. Fear is a dark and distorted glass. Yet every aspect of ego perception has a counterpart in truth that is pure and beautiful. For every loveless thought, for every cruel or misguided motive, for every arrogance within, there is a gentler view already made to take its place and to deliver a healing in exchange.

The perceptual dream is like a shattered mirror. What we see in it is incomplete and highly distorted. Love puts the pieces back together and presents our mind with a picture that accurately reflects the real world and therefore gladdens our heart. It is not important how this is done, but it is all important that we want it done. "Do I want to see other people as lacking or as whole?" "Do I want to be justified, or do I want the world to have deep and lasting peace?" "Do I want small advantages or complete freedom?" "Do I want love or fear?" Only our heart's answer to these questions controls the time of our awakening. And nothing external can hinder it.

Summary: You are asleep. Yet God, your higher Self, is awake within you and is all around you. Even in sleep you can hear what is entirely You. Therefore, listen to God.

COMMUNICATION

Strictly speaking, we do not communicate; we allow communication to be. Peace—not attempts to change, overcome, or break through—opens wide the channels of understanding and acceptance and love. Communication is actually a stepping back from effort. It is a moment's rest from needs. This gentle contentment permits an extension of our thoughts to others through a simultaneous welcoming of theirs.

Any self-image, held up in thought, interferes with natural relating. We cannot orchestrate our performance and still see clearly to whom we are speaking. Prideful announcements, compliments, verbal talents used to set us apart, "kind" words motivated by guilt, attacks on third parties, controversial pronouncements, "constructive" criticisms, and questions meant to highlight another's error cannot be communicated because they will not be accepted in happiness and wholly shared. As best we can, we must permit one whole, lovely, softly illuminated idea of God to encompass all parties. We settle back into enjoyment and choose only to be free.

The ego's answer to verbal conflict is to quickly provide you with grounds for being right. This may lend a temporary sense of increase, but only in one spot. No sense of joining will accompany it, and the apparently larger "size" of your ego will soon appear hopelessly small against the universe with which you are now at odds. If you feel a stab of anxiety as you start to speak, you have defined another as different from yourself. Remember that your body does not **have** to express this decision to attack.

Nor is verbal agreement an answer, because it can be, and often is, only superficial. The heart of the question will not have been satisfied if we merely adopt a different stance. Is there anything truly opposed to us if all things proceed from Love Itself? Certainly there appear to be many dangers, and numerous the ones who stand in the way of our safety. But what can stand before the light if all is Light? Both perceptions cannot be accurate. Our work is a simple choice between the two. Either we determine to see innocence or cherish guilt. The choice is only difficult as long as we insist on exceptions. We all walk together for good. What each one says is true because the truth of God is in him. There is a way of seeing that. We stand **behind** his eyes and look out. Now we feel his fears as our own and know that in his release is our freedom as well.

Our objective is a simple and direct one. In conversation we seek an experience, not an intellectual exchange. We want to help and make happy. The verbal form this takes is irrelevant. To attempt correction of another is to insist that his fault is real. The universe contains no mistakes, and our insistence that it does can only depress us. Instead, we focus on an exchange of love and drop our ego's expectation that our gifts be treated with respect. We gently walk around any opportunity offered to feel separate from the person before us. Silently, we join with his spirit, which is an actual part of God and therefore of our Self. We wait for the eternal communication that is now occurring to dawn on our awareness, knowing it will become apparent once we have cleared a quiet spot within us where it can be heard and felt.

A helpful approach to communication does not differ from a practical attitude toward any other situation or condition: love works; attack does not. If you were in prayer and an angry thought crossed your mind, you would not delay your communion with God by engaging in a private analysis of it or in a long refutation. You would simply open it to the light of day and quickly turn your attention back to God. When we are with another, we are in a potential state of prayer with God. That is why we cannot hide our thoughts and still be in full communication with those around us.

Bodies are our ideas given form. This is true whether we are seeing them physically, in fantasies, or in dreams. To endlessly argue with another body is only to deceive ourselves that one of our judgments has disconnected itself from our mind and has become a separate entity that can distract our attention from Love.

We believe what we want to, but we see only what we believe. Choice operates on the level of our desires. We are free to believe what is occurring in truth or to make for ourselves another interpretation, but once decided, the outpicturing of this wish is automatic.

When the mind engages in idle wishing, it is really **exercising** a particular set of beliefs. This becomes our silent affirmation of how we want our lives to be. We may, for example, fantasize mock conversations in order to produce the feeling that our positions are right and those of others wrong. Being "right" is the gift offered us by the ego to turn from trust to distrust. But in this turning we turn from God also and from our Self.

An effective way to deal with this type of mental mis-activity is to ask, "What do I **want** to believe about my current relationships?" For what we believe is what we will experience. Do we **want** a life of confrontations? Do we really want new opportunities for personal vindication?

Our own replays of past incidents and our imagining of future ones affirm that we do. Rest from this misuse of our mind affirms we do not. Recognizing that we have chosen mistakenly, we choose again. This time we release all people from their roles as destroyers of our peace. And we can make the same internal choice in the middle of an "actual" confrontation. We simply rest from judging anyone. We fail completely to give an interpretation to another's motives, knowing that God alone assigns each one's role and function. Instead, we allow a blessing to settle over all we see and hear. And we wait in love for a new appreciation to be given us.

Because we recognize that we are perceiving a relationship as a problem, our first step is to undo the order we have imposed on the components of the situation. How we have set things up must be relinquished before we can find ourselves in a position to see all the parts arranged differently. The way we presently have others classified actually prevents solution of the difficulties between us. So we forego our descriptions and acknowledge that it would be better if we were wrong. Turning to God, we say in all honesty that we are unable to instruct ourselves how to respond to this person, and then we listen for Love's gentle Answer. We always hear the Answer when we become as quiet as the Answer Itself.

The rule for successful communication is **attempt to share only ideas that will be received by the other person with all of his heart.** An opposing thought will not and cannot be communicated. Once it is recognized that nothing is accomplished by attempting to correct another, the ego will frequently retreat to a new position: "I am not trying to dictate his role, but he is trying to dictate mine. I am willing to forgive him, but he continues to judge everything I do." The suggestion here is that somehow the other person should pick up on what we are attempting and do the same.

It is as simple to forgive unforgiveness as it is any other mistake. You **have** this person's internal cooperation, and the miracle that awaits you depends on this unalterable fact. You are not special. You are equal in unending perfection and limitless freedom. God is our Identity.

We will never gain another's undivided external cooperation, because for us to see someone as external is to believe that his interests cannot be identical to ours. The solution is to stop fighting that appearance, no matter what form it takes, and mentally seek out the love-self within him. Love recognizes its own. Love sees a different set of interests because it looks beyond behavior and past personal history into the deep urges for goodness which unite us with others from within.

The only goal we need have in any relationship is to sense a quiet presence within. This is indeed a happy pursuit. The light of God does shine. It is our welcome Home. There is only one Friend in all our friends. It is only His gentle assurance that we look for. We deceive ourselves whenever we think an improvement has occurred in the outward situation. We can monitor only our internal state without hurting ourselves. We seek no confirmation except an increased sense of God's presence. And this is always received quietly. It comes with our wish for peace, held lovingly in thought, and extended to all. We are engaged in putting ourselves back together. Our sight has been shattered, but not the fact of our Oneness. Each person we encounter appears to hold a lost piece of us. It joins with us the instant it is recognized. And love is the way to see it.

SPECIAL AREAS
OF PRACTICE

MONEY

We cannot hold tightly to a sense of private ownership and control and still act in peace toward all others. Nor can we turn control over to another body and find freedom by denying responsibility. We are responsible for everything because we are everything. But only in God can we see what that means.

Either God can be trusted with our needs or He cannot. God is not reliable **sometimes**. Erratic trustworthiness is meaningless. To first decide what we want and then look to God as a means to get it is partial or meaningless trust. In God alone we recognize both our need and its answer. He directs us in all things, but He cannot be used to eliminate the anxiety we feel when we consult Him only partially.

God can plan for our happiness and provide for our safety. But have we demonstrated an equal ability? Is it not clear there is a part of our mind we are not trusting? Love is our food and shelter, not merely the means of obtaining them, and in this recognition are all temporary needs met. There is neither abundance nor scarcity in dreams. There are only illusions. To seek more illusions, or to pride ourselves on having fewer, keeps us attached to the hopeless process of trading one form of emptiness for another.

The number of things we own or the number of years we live do not attest to our spiritual advancement any more than scarcity adds respectability to the body that experiences it. Since we own nothing we cannot presume what to do with it. Only by relinquishing our small and bitter authority will we wake in Love and know the freedom that comes from trusting everything. Nothing less than All will ever satisfy us.

Possibly this much can be safely generalized about money:

> No one should be denied our help because he cannot pay. And we should be equally open to giving money as to receiving it.

> We should not spend money out of fear, nor need we assume that the aim in all we do is to save money. Our aim is to be guided Home. God can **not** be "bothered" by too small a question. He wants His children to have peace.

> Neither wealth nor poverty should be sought to enhance our self-image. **All** self-images are of the ego.

Obtaining money should never become our priority. That limited a goal will not heal us. By making the heeding of His guidance our first objective, we will recognize just how safe it is to leave the future in His hands.

SEX

The deep yearning we sometimes feel for a physical relationship has within it a yearning that is deeper still. We are not at home in a body, and we are not fully and unwaveringly wanted by any other body. Yet we do have a home, and we have an endless welcome there. It is that for which we yearn.

Even though we may mistakenly interpret a spiritual impulse as being physical, that mistake is not a sin. And it is not necessarily the most helpful approach to fight the symptoms of that mistake, whether they take the form of mastur-bation, promiscuity, a conflicted "sex-life" within a marriage, homosexuality, or any of a thousand other forms of behavior. The wish to "sin" and the means we use to pursue that wish are not the same. Only our goal to sin can hurt us, but God can show us a new use for every means we now employ. We have not yet been asked to not see the body, but only to see it in a way that will allow us to be happy. Your present way may call for great sacrifice and depression, and that is not necessary. The desire to have what you want will always deprive you. Desire only to have what you have, and you will come to see that you have everything there is or could ever be.

The body is the part of our mind we think is not mind but is something else. We therefore treat it as something else. It appears to have separated itself from the rest and become an end or goal in itself. The only solution to the resulting confusion and pain is to treat what is mind as mind. It is to extend what was meant to be extended and not meant to be a stopping point. The attempt to stop love is pain. To use the body only as a way of communicating love restores the body to the mind and ends pain. Nothing short of kindness feels good.

There are three guidelines that will save time in most instances. One should not, on his own, attempt to eliminate an outward form of relating that has become common to a relationship. For example, one should not insist on abstinence from sexual intercourse with his spouse under the assumption that abstinence is more loving. Conversely, one should not attempt to influence another into having sex, or into beginning a new form of sexual practice, if that person is not so inclined at the moment. How frequently two people have physical contact indicates nothing about the strength of their relationship. And how infrequently an individual expresses himself sexually does not relate to his spirituality.

The mere behavior of a body is never spiritual. And so the third guideline is as follows: Fighting against any aspect of behavior we have identified with will not of itself lessen that identification. We cannot improve the ego; we can only relinquish it.

How to free ourselves from painful pleasures and short-lived gratifications does not have to be guessed. Nor can it be solved through endless examination and analyzation. Only Light gives light. We cannot produce it by ourselves because light is the recognition that we are not by ourselves. The longing for other bodies is grounded in the deeply held belief that we are merely a solitary body and not the extension of God.

Be gentle with yourself, for gentleness is of God, your Father. And in that attitude of kindliness and true helpfulness, God will come to you and lead you past sexual problems and a thousand other hindrances you did not recognize, all at the same instant.

CHILDREN

We make the same mistake in every situation that becomes a problem. Once again we have deceived ourselves that we are encountering a thing that is not like us. This applies whether we are dealing with "city hall" or the "terrible twos." The final answer will not lie in isolating one aspect of the situation and trying to force a change. When relating to children, our goal remains to enter into the realm of peace just beyond the picture seen with our senses. And nothing short of this entry will be an accomplishment that will bring us rest.

Each stage of development our child enters is another opportunity to respond to the part of him that will not change. Only the eternal can be related to, communicated with, entered, and joined in full cooperation. Our ego will argue that our "new" child calls for still another definition of ourself as parent. If we adjust by merely changing our self-image, we will not stop perceiving our interests as different from our child's, and we will still have ample evidence of opposing minds, wills, emotions, and conflicting rights to time and property. We cannot begin by believing we are a parent and expect to have within our experience the evidence of one Self.

Whenever feasible, our initial response to a child's unexpected behavior should be inner quietness and openness. Only an instant is needed. This is a new habit that rehabituates the mind. The old reactions of anger and of fear of not being liked are turned from in preference to a new response of immediate joining with the Source of our answer. A still and gentle mind cannot be cruel.

The way Home for both us and our children is approach through attraction. It is a path of gifts leading to the final gift. The experience of Heaven begins with "yes." "No" merely marks the places where happiness cannot be found under any circumstances. It is a temporary means, but it is not a sufficient communication to lead us safely forward. The rule is, **once your child understands that you mean "no," he will accept it as his own answer.** "No" is not properly a warning of our intention to attack. It is a firm, safe, unmovable buffer against what will hurt someone with the understanding of a child. As parents, we allow our child to come up against it, until, in his own time, he realizes the buffer will not move. However, he must also realize that **we** are not what will hurt him. That is why it is not necessary to intensify the factors he is afraid of in order to change his behavior.

Our goal is not to modify behavior but to clarify communication. We are not against our children and therefore do not attempt to teach them fear. We are **for** harmlessness and invulnerability.

At times, our consistency may seem to be taking the form of out-enduring our own children. This approach is an improvement on anger, but it is improved still further when mere endurance is reinterpreted into gentle, change-less patience. As parents, we are content to wait, remaining very firm, but not dangerous, until our child changes his mind. Our "no" is now a form of watching over him to keep him safe.

Never allow the question to become, "What am I going to do about it if my child defies me?" Our objective as parents is not to defend our pride. That would be to teach pride. Nor is our goal to communicate disapproval. Scissors, knives, matches, and other things a baby does not understand must be taken from him even though he may scream his misinterpretation of our intention to make him safe and happy. But an older child does not have to be put in pain or banished from his favorite place in order to "pay" for what he has done.

A simple "Do only this" is easier for a child to understand than abstract explanations of what he should not do because of how it will en-danger him. Teach approach, not avoidance.

Teach love, not fear. Teach simplicity and clarity. Allow your thoughts and actions to fit what your child **is**, and do not do anything out of fear of what your child may become. Show him his unchanging source of reward, not a thousand shifting shadows. Give him one clear instruction that will never fail to guide him safely and happily. It is not words we teach or learn, it is an experience. Therefore, enfold your child in your experience of generosity, of release, of gentle perspective, and of sweet lightheartedness, until you see his interests as yours, and yours as his, and only Love as the Parent of us all.

MARRIAGE

Whom God has joined, nothing can threaten, and all the Family of God is one in peace. The marriage ceremony symbolizes a preexistent state. It is one of many symbols. Marriage celebrates the happy, eternal fact of the unity of all life and the exclusion of none. In marrying, those who are one acknowledge their Oneness.

Marriage does not have to be worked at, but our perception of the State it symbolizes does have to be guarded. Our "work" is merely to give endless welcome to all the seemingly scattered evidences of Oneness. **Marriage need only continue unresisted.** We can interfere with our recognition of it, but we can hardly separate ourselves from another of God's children. There is only one Self.

Relationships are our primary means of awaking. The times we set aside for prayer and meditation would appear to be our best opportunities to commune with God, but if these are still too closely associated with physical isolation, we may fail to see the light in others that constitutes the answer to our prayer.

As the light of truth begins to dawn in

thought, the student of God may suddenly have the uncanny experience of seeing others as himself. A moment may come when he recognizes that he is literally them. This makes no sense on a perceptual level, but it makes perfect sense on the level of love. Now there is no boundary to his prayer, for he sees that he has nothing to lose from another's gain. Others' joy is his in truth.

The level on which only egos encounter can be depressing and fearful. As it is seen more honestly, it may appear to become increasingly dark. To someone consciously attempting to wake in Love, this melting of the candy shell that covers some forms of murder can be very distressing and may be misinterpreted as his personal failure.

There are two steps in seeing the light of God. What is dark must be recognized as without light, and light must be seen as harmless and desirable. No compromise in this distinction is possible, for to continue to accommodate darkness is to want another experience besides love.

If value is believed to reside in any form of confrontation, love will appear to be a highly unstable component of all relationships. In your communications, emphasize no thought or feeling within you except gentleness. Only through gentleness can you remain fully open and accessible, and unless you are open, you **will** try to hurt others to protect what you believe must remain secret. Therefore, hold no part of you separate. Seek no private thoughts. Be completely transparent and harmless.

If we are ever to know love without limits, there can be no range to our giving. To want something from another is to utterly misunderstand his role in our happiness. Another person is our opportunity to extend what we **are**. Other bodies are not our means of proving we are incomplete and in need. That is why attempts to strike deals often set in place a deterrent to free communication and peaceful relating. Whoever understands this at the moment must assume responsibility for whatever is occurring in the marriage. One person, making the effort to forgive completely what is happening and to replace his own anxiety and criticisms with a gentle lightheartedness and limitless goodwill, will become the governing factor in any relationship he is part of.

It is not necessary to encourage our spouse to talk about what we judge to be wrong with the marriage or to talk about anything at all. It is not necessary to pressure our spouse to take responsibility for his part or to confess his mistakes. It is not necessary to force compromises or to formulate a joint plan of external response to future problems. Nothing is really necessary except that we remind ourselves alone that we are not in this relationship by accident and that all that occurs **can** be seen in love. A kind vision is always a possibility. It will occur when one person pauses long enough to recall his heartfelt thanks for how central a role the other person has played in his spiritual growth, whether the other person consciously intended this effect or not.

Because all minds are in full communication, one happy, forgiving, restful thought will of itself extend throughout all areas of a marriage. Nothing exists that can actually stand in the way of this expansion. To accept full responsibility for everything and guilt for nothing is true humility and the certain road to success.

HEALING

Healing is return to normal. It is therefore completely natural. Once again, we function as we
were meant to. In all we think and see we are
whole, deeply satisfied, richly happy and free.
The miracle **does** nothing because healing is a
fact and disease is mere interference.

It is reasonable to assume that sickness is an
attempt to keep ourselves in an unnatural position. Our mind has grabbed tightly onto
something foreign. Yet this is not reason for
self-censure or shame any more than "good"
health is our personal accomplishment. We are
truly healthy only when we do not feel or see
sickness anywhere. Healing "occurs" when we
allow our minds to return to a wholly innocent
and peaceful way of seeing.

Even though illness is a decision, there can be
aids to choosing again. It is possible to look
honestly at any difficulty and recognize that it
holds nothing we want. If that degree of honesty
is not feasible at the moment, there are many
ways to build within us a greater love of truth.

Disease is a form of fear, so to release the
mind of fear is to return to health. Following a

strict policy of foregoing all medicine and other physical means of healing is not always the path to a genuine reduction in fear. These decisions should not be made without the aid of internal guidance. God's voice within us is a better consultant than the memory of an old position we may have now outgrown. Love is always a **present** help in troubled times.

If you feel guided by Love to try a mental approach to healing your own body, your chances of success will be increased if you remain open to any advice, whether medical, "natural," or spiritual, that your inner Physician suggests. Only God heals, and only the mind is truly healed. The delusion that we have personal healing powers, or have been singled out by God for certain divine gifts, can delay our way Home more than would a moment's pain. Yet when we are still, there is no limit at all on what God can do through us.

As the student continues on his way, he may quite unexpectedly "develop" certain abilities. For example, it may appear that if he does a particular thing, says or thinks certain words, those around him find themselves well. So he will not delay himself and others, it is important that he recognize just what it is about all of this that does not matter. Physical change, without an accompanying release from fear, does not matter. It is neither good nor bad. Love is the only miracle, and if we do something that tempts another into thinking Love is external and peculiar to some other body, we have impoverished him and ourselves.

Any external healing agent is a form of magic. But that does not mean it should never be employed. As in all things, we protect our minds from deception when we turn to God for instructions on how to proceed. If you are able to "heal" through touching, mental imagery, silent "treatments," physical repositioning, colors, sounds, or by advocating the use of devices, machines, diet, or movement, that ability does not **have** to be put to use. Allow God to tell you when to use it and when not to. It is not **always** kind to remove pain by offering dependency in its place. Show another his unfailing and internal source of Help.

IMAGERY

Your body is a teaching aid. It is like a screen on which all your thoughts are pictured. If you have failed to forgive yourself, this attack will be symbolically manifested in some form of physical distress. Step back from your body and pretend to attack it in the exact manner necessary to produce the distress, and perhaps you will see what you are angry with yourself about. Anger is not your ally, and it is certainly not a form of humility. Now step back again. You **are** the light of God that enters and purifies. Gently shine away every tension in your mind and body. This is your part to play. By merely attempting this you make the effort God has asked you to make, and the "results" are of no interest to you whatsoever.

Forgiveness heals, for it allows every form of assault to pass from thought. This process can be quietly pictured as easily as said:

EXAMPLE: Because God wants you to be happy, you can give Him no greater gift than one of your sorrows. See God, your Protector, waiting patiently beside you for you to ask His help. Each time you notice anger or anything at all that distresses you, wrap it as a present and hold it out to Him. As He takes it and shines it all away, feel His deep thanks that you have allowed Him to lighten your burden and expand your joy.

Place your pains and censures and all your old forebodings in a container of your choosing. Make up a way for it to be transported from your attention and your life.

Using rain, a breeze, the purifying sunlight, or the soft flow of a river, permit your hurts to dissolve and be carried away. With only what God made left behind, see how you sparkle now, clean and pure, the object of His endless love.

EXAMPLE: Before you is a waterfall, heavenly in its beauty. It pours like love from the Heart of God. Divest yourself of all your worries and stand for a while undefended in its gentle downpour. Each tiny aspect of you is cleaned throughout, and now you emerge in total newness, brilliant in your harmlessness toward everything.

Stillness heals, because only an active mind can hallucinate. Here are some ways of visualizing stillness:

You may rub in the deep hush of God's presence into every patch of soreness or hate. Watch the balm of peace remove completely what was never there.

Pour into the damaged parts of the body a healing oil. Let it settle there like silence and spread like the gift of grace.

Or float a blanket of God's quiet snow over each form of fear. Watch those areas of the body relax in His enveloping safety and care.

EXAMPLE: See floating down to you a lovely parachute. It carries a can of celestial paint marked "The Peace of God." You dip the attached brush into the silvery liquid and softly spread it over every difficulty, until the landscape of your mind and body comes to rest.

Blessing heals, for we can give what we have received in full. We can bless our body, which represents our present concept of ourself, far more effortlessly than we can curse it. And we can safely use the name and bodily image of another as the subject of our need to forgive and be fair.

Direct a light into any place you see fearful shadows. Mentally rest your hand over this area and focus Love's warmth into the troubled spot.

Let healing occur by visualizing a specific thing that represents your love, surrounding, replacing, or comforting the places that hurt. Or, using the sounds or the colors you hold dear, change the present tone to one of harmony.

Within your mind, touch the pain with a holy object. Or erase it with a sacred substance. Or see God's Hand releasing and comforting all the areas of upset in you or in another.

EXAMPLE: Draw a circle of light around you. Fill in every shadow and all the empty spaces with light of equal brilliance. Now switch yourself on and see that **you** are the light of this circle. Then draw your circle around the world, and see clearly that you are also the light of the world. Behold its brilliance arching above you and the splendor of its beauty below and all about. Rest in this vision for a peaceful moment. For the truth will not hurt you.

Entering the Place of God will certainly heal you, for your house and His are one:

EXAMPLE: Travel to a spot where you would love to be. Or transport another there. Any kind of place you wish to picture. Smell its perfumes and hear its gentle sounds. Leave all types of attack far behind and watch for a while only the surroundings you enjoy. Now comes your special Guardian. The happy sight of him is familiar. He is answering your call. In his hand he holds the thing you have asked for. Take it and let it heal whatever troubles there are. And thank him by giving relief in your mind and heart to all the world.

Summary   If you arrange for elements of conflict in your images, you are still cherishing some kind of attack within your life. That is why changing the body should never become a goal that substitutes for true healing. Healing is merely peace, and occurs wholly within your mind. And all of the above suggestions are meant only to bring light to your mind, for your body is a reflection. The body is never a reasonable object of your concern. It simply pictures thought. Nothing threatening can be contained in what only represents a condition within your control.

A consistently restful and comforting approach to mental change will reflect the same throughout your body and relationships, and in every other aspect of your life. Make your imagery games as harmless and free of conflict as God's power Itself. You do not have to fight anything. You **are** love. Picture what delights and relaxes you, and hear only what lifts you to joy. Sing a quiet song to your mind that will transform each strain of sadness you identify. Dance your thoughts in its music, and let there be dirges no more.

HONESTY

To the ego there appears to be a conflict between a harmless intention and the goal of honesty. However, honesty is not complete as long as certain contents of the mind are being emphasized. A peaceful mind is at rest with all its parts. Gentleness responds to everything equally because it responds to everything fully. To fear no exposure of any kind is to become instantly harmless.

Forget what you have judged is needed and let yourself say what you say. How can you be certain of the outcome your words will lead to? Therefore, forget words and wish well. If the world would do only this one thing—hide nothing—there would be peace between people forevermore.

It is such a relief to hide nothing. Yet this relief will not be gained by our attempting to make our body and behavior so perfect that not a thing would remain to embarrass us. Embarrassments do not matter. As long as we retain an ego, it will attack our motives and judge against the body that acted as their agent. There is no love and consequently no freedom from fear in an ego. Only by consistently hiding nothing do we eventually relinquish the ego, because it is merely the mind's idle wish to remain apart.

Hold back no part of you and you will not attack. Openness does not contain the need to rehearse in advance what is to be said or done. It defers judgment, and therefore guilt, altogether. Honesty is another name for generosity.

It may not be apparent at first that the desire to analyze another's motives and deliver a "just" response is dishonest and secretive. Yet this much should be obvious: love is being concealed and avoided. When no attempt is made to rank in importance one's emotions and thoughts, the contents of the mind merge, and light is the residual. All forms of darkness are merely shadow feelings. They contain nothing that is not imagined. Honesty is the coming of truth, which dispells without effort and without attack that which is not true. The truth, in whatever form it takes, is your friend. Trust it. Openness, pure and simple, is the only thing you ever need.

FORGIVENESS

The existence of now gains credence as we
journey toward it. More and more frequently it
breaks into consciousness. Gradually we come
to trust it as we would trust a friend of perfect
faithfulness. And whenever it is chosen over
absentmindedness, for an instant the perceptual
world fades and all we ever wanted is seen to be
at hand. Yet when we look at all there is to be
done, we cannot help feeling defeated before we
even begin. How can we use the body harm-
lessly at all times? How can we look at another
without recalling his past actions and holding
these limitations against him? How can we free
our minds of fear? How can we fail to value
another for his specialness alone? The answer is
we cannot meet any of these goals in the days
to come. To forgive another for all time seems
impossible, but to forgive him for just one instant—this instant—is fully within our capa-
bility. Whenever we release our mind from a
condemnatory train of thought and allow it to
return to gentleness, we are practicing pure
forgiveness. To rest from judgment is to absolve
from guilt. Anyone can direct his thoughts to

Love for one moment. It is true that the very next moment he may again yield to temptation. But that will not really matter because it will not truly be the "next" moment. It will always remain now, and now will still be the lesson he is learning. "Am I willing to love, to forgive, to bless, to heal for just one instant?" is a question that addresses itself to reality. "How will I be able to do this tomorrow?" questions a person who is not here and a time that is not now. Say instead, "I am here. I am only now. And God is all that has happened."

A BENEDICTION

You stand at the Source looking out. You are blessed, and you can extend an endless blessing. Close your eyes and imagine this happy scene of healing. You are a stream that has begun to flow in an old and dry bed. You are a bringer of cool water to earth that is parched and dead. In your wake seeds sprout up and bloom. The earth turns to life at your coming. From this time on you may offer a cup of cool water to everyone you meet or think about, to those yet to come, and to those who have been here and left. You may offer it in joy and ask nothing in payment. You need not preach or exhort. You need not ignore or disdain. You may safely offer all you have so that you may have still more of its Source, of which you are a part. You offer a simple choice, an alternative to bitterness and despair. And because you stand in God, you see all things in His light. Nothing before you deserves to suffer. No one is unworthy of His help. You extend Love's light to an earth that turns willingly to receive the light. You stand in God. You stand in Love. You offer light to shine away the cold shadows of fear.

You offer, but you do not manipulate or force. You stand in God, and you feel His gratitude pour through you with each one who accepts His gifts. Resolve to remain as constant in your giving as is your Source, until that time comes when every living thing will wake to its innocence and find itself at Home.

The world will end in joy, because it is a place of sorrow. When joy has come, the purpose of the world has gone. The world will end in peace, because it is a place of war. When peace has come, what is the purpose of the world? The world will end in laughter, because it is a place of tears. Where there is laughter, who can longer weep? And only complete forgiveness brings all this to bless the world. In blessing it departs, for it will not end as it began. To turn hell into Heaven is the function of God's teachers, for what they teach are lessons in which Heaven is reflected. And now sit down in true humility, and realize that all God would have you do you can do. Do not be arrogant and say you cannot learn His Own curriculum. His Word says otherwise. His Will be done. It cannot be otherwise. And be you thankful it is so.

A Course in Miracles